FOREWORD

The concurrence of the international community in setting a specific date to end extreme poverty is most proactive, responsive and reassuring. The World Bank has declared 2030 to end poverty. This is in congruence with the United Nations 2030's mark to accomplish the Sustainable Development Goals (SDGs), a continuum of the Millennium Development Goals (MDGs), whose top on goals is ending extreme poverty. Multiple forces against this cankerworm are justified because of the latter's infamous complexity. Indeed, poverty is a multivariate function because enormous undesirable indices positively correlate with it. But, the good news is that development agencies have now poverty reduction as their chief targets.

The stuff of what the book, 'Growing Robust Economy' is made of is catechizing and apt. And for us here robust economy is a passionate vision, to ensure food sustainability and wellbeing for citizenries. I am particularly impressed by the author's style and diction, and it has proved true that he has grasps of the workings of the development sector.

The holistic robust economy will be optimally achieved when each entity of the development sector pursues with vigour implementation of economy-growing strategies. As the author penned down in this treaties, reinvigorating the economic nodes assures improved activities and better outcomes. But before that is done, understanding the dynamics of the economic systems is as critical to afford better insight as to what strategies to adopt. The vision of transformation has made it pertinent to concentrate on the infrastructural and productive sectors of the economy.

Therefore, the enablers of policy underpinnings of government must be strengthened to integrate growth engine into economic systems. In the health sector, for example, framework realignment is essential to maintain robust community-based Primary Healthcare Service Delivery System, through provision of comprehensive health care service and health insurance scheme, with the view to achieving an effective institutionalized routine immunization.

Equally, governments must be interested in education, agriculture and other real sectors of the economy. New technologies in agriculture should be adapted and hatched into the agribusiness potentials. Education should be wedded into the industrial needs of the economy, to enable optimal performance of the Micro Small and Medium Scale Enterprises (MSMEs). As MSMEs provide driving force to sustainable industrialization, the revitalization of manpower and skills potentials of labour resource is strategic in realising a well-coordinated growth pattern.

A people oriented government takes cognizance of efficient performance of government organs, and indeed other organizations, on which it largely underlie, as the latent energies of Public Private Partnership (PPP) are exploited.

Dr P. Chinatu Njoku
General Manager, Abia CSDP

PREFACE

A solution to newly appearing economic problems... often cannot be based on existing methods but needs new ideas and approaches.

Leonid V. Kantorovich (1912-1986)
1975 winner of Nobel Memorial Prize in Economic Sciences

Economic doldrums, in the form of depression or stagflation, have intermittently lingered in and out of geographical locations in a random pattern across the globe. In aggregation, therefore, they have persisted. As such, the world may be rightly termed as not being able to command a universal economic prosperity, apart from parches of economic surpluses in one country and the converse at the other. And the booms, if you have observed, rarely last; paving way for the regular downturns.

It, as such, has raised questions as to the best approach to be adopted to ensure robust economy amid the impeding downturns. The robustness of economy goes beyond nominal economic realities but entrenched in the psyche and resilience of the fabrics of the systems. The acquisition of skills and the quality of skills in terms of versatility and turgidity is critical to the robustness of the economy. The stabilizers as economic mechanisms to avoid boom (avert inflation) and avoid depression (avert doldrums) have been effective but do not guarantee robustness of economies, in the real sense of the term.

Therefore, this text has been able to look at the efficacy of industrial-cluster practice as an economic approach, expansionary outlook and attitudinal renewal as an enduring mechanism to achieve economic stability of nations. The former is key in expanding the economic assets while the latter turns around the perception of the countries to enable radiation of modernisation necessary for sustainable development and industrialization. This discourse however zeroes in on the industrial-cluster model and its merits.

It has to be clearly stated, that there is no geographical location that is not endowed with resources enough to grow their prosperity. God was faithful about that at creation and that followed the declaration in the book of Romans that the creatures are waiting for the manifestation of the sons of God to harness their endowments. Countries like Japan and China apparently had less to be desired in terms of natural resources, but the lean resources were turned around. They believed in the ability to activate their latent reserves for wealth creation, thus they pursued such with vigour and now they are in the G7 and G20.

Singapore hiked from poor country, less than half a century ago after they gained sovereignty in 1965, all the way to a high-income economy on the planet earth with very high Human Development Index (HDI); so also Brazil. Similarly, after the Second World War Israel was literally chaperoned to their land through the United Nations Partition Plan adopted in 1947 and subsequent independence in 1948, and they were left with the only option of conquering their environment and challenges to reclaim their heritage, today they are in the OECD. The State of Israel has the second-largest number of start-ups, after the United States.

What these countries did was to re-discover where they possessed comparative advantages and harnessed them. They defied the ordinary and went the extra-ordinary way to achieve their aims. Nigeria, as a country, is heavily endowed with agricultural resources, human resources, mineral resources, forestry and wild resources, traditional and tourism resources, and market resources. At optimization of her full potentials, the country would represent seedbed for human resource development and a preferred tourists' haven.

However, in achieving this, necessary preliminary framework action needs to be done, notably the needs assessment executed through market research survey and analysis. Market research survey is a test on taste; it is a process that helps to understand customers' habits, likes and dislikes, get product feedback and measure brand awareness etcetera. This strategy broadened at national level, commodities with high utility and price elasticity of demand should be focussed on through industrial-cluster approach to energize the commercial climate.

In growing sustainable and scalable economies, particularization of the development cradles is imperative. The policy of supporting the MSMEs in industrial melting-pots is pristine because of their vibrancy and high business birthing. Whereas Aba is known for trading, another of its major mainstay is craftsmanship, especially, in leather works, the sitting of leather production cluster and possible invitation of conglomerates with tenacity and track-record of this production will be germane.

This step, partly, is a creative response to the nation-wide economic recession. In fact, it is bi-focal in nature; cushioning the effect of economic downturn and re-establishing the nation as a commercial hub of the West African Region. The new dawn of investors' drive and partnership for industrial cluster reflects an opening to wide opportunity of innovativeness and industrialization, and assurance for greater Nigeria.

The government policy on agriculture will adequately serve the MSMEs sub-sector, through the supply of raw materials. The agribusiness segment would provide semi-finished products to the factories. The huge natural resources are critical to feeding the industries whose functions they are to transform these farm produce. Research could go into these farm outputs to unveil their industrial values, in order to fuse them into the production chain. When that is done, the sky is the limit for Nigeria's economic expansion as the unemployment rate will plummet.

Then, a robust economy would have been grown.

Anozie G. Nwokoma
November, 2019

ABBREVIATIONS

AfDB:	African Development Bank
BPP:	Bureau of Public Procurement
CDD:	Community Driven Development
CPAR:	Country Procurement Assessment Review
CSDP	Community and Social Development Project
QCBS:	Quality and Cost Based Selection
CQS:	Selection Based on the Consultants' Qualification
DC:	Direct Contracting
DOX:	Design of Experience
EFCC:	Economic and Financial Crimes Commission
EOIs:	Expressions of Interest
FA:	Framework Agreement
FfP:	Fit-for-Purpose
HDI:	Human Development Index
IBRD:	International Bank for Reconstruction and Development
IC:	Individual Consultancy
ICB:	International Competitive Bidding
ICC:	International Chamber of Commerce
ICPC:	Independent Corrupt Practices Commission
ICSID:	International Centre for Settlement of Investment Disputes
ICT:	Information and Communication Technology
IDA:	International Development Association
IFB:	Invitation for Bids
IFIs:	International Financing Institutions
IGR:	Internally Generated Revenue
IT:	Information Technology
ITB:	Instruction to Bidders
ITC:	Instruction to Consultants
LC:	Letter of Credit

LCS: Least Cost Selection
LGAs   Local Government Areas
MDAs: Ministries, Departments and Agencies
MDBs: Multilateral Development Banks
MSMEs: Micro, Small and Medium Scale Enterprises
MIGA: Multilateral Investment Guarantee Agency
NAFDAC: National Agency for Food and Drug
                Administration and Control
NCB: National Competitive Bidding
NEWMAP: Nigeria Erosion and Watershed
                Management Project
NS: National Shopping
OECD: Organization for Economic Corporation and
                Development
PDO: Project Development Objective
PPF: Project Preparation Facility
PPP: Public and Private Partnership
SDGs: Sustainable Development Goals
SOEs: Statement of Expenditures
SON: Standard Organization of Nigeria
SWOT: Strength-Weakness-Opportunity-Threat
VAT: Value Added Tax
VfM: Value for Money

CHAPTER 1

An Overview Of Industrial Cluster Concept

Manufacturers' location of firms, and indeed other economic units, has been, for centuries, a thing of keen and diligent consideration. At global level, governments talk and aspire for an enabling environment in order to attract foreign direct investment; so also corporations and other production outfits that seek vibrant environment to optimize their performance metrics.

Particularly speaking, in planning for location of industries, entrepreneurs envision such benefits accrued from nearness to sources of raw materials, availability of skilled manpower, proximity and reliability of power sources, existence of access roads, accessibility of micro-financings, and tax incentivization. In an economic climate characterized by lean resources, these are obviously objects that determine the reality of profit maximization, hence the need for similar industries to be located in a place to enable one-service-for-all. The approach of industrial cluster framework becomes more efficient. Indeed, industrial cluster approach has passed its litmus test in industrialization process in Aba, Abia State of Nigeria, for example.

Now, localization is a policy framework in economic firmament with key outlook of closeness to the market. The viability of providing financing to entrepreneurs in cluster framework has proven effective because the webbed membership makes it difficult for default scenarios. The social inclusivity steers the spirit that retain

faith on achievement. More so, the positive externalities, which the pull effect (agglomeration effect) generate are very profitable. This concept definitely pulls necessary inducement for the government to have confidence in the members of the cluster, as have been witnessed in Abia State that enabled the government to send members of the shoe makers' cluster to China to enhance their skills and boost productivity.

It is eureka for Abia State, having achieved breakthrough through this initiative, which has resulted in the high productivity that enable high volume sales of shoe and fabric products to the armed forces and the paramilitary agencies in the country.

The Cluster Concept is not entirely a new policy, as Nigerian nation had in the past promoted the setting up of industrial estates. This initiative was in view of finding solution to industrial development challenges.

Along this line, government identified the major challenges of industry to include unstable infrastructure, which cannot sustain meaningful and competitive economic activities; lack of enabling environment for business development, particularly in terms of multiple taxation, inadequate incentives and absence of credit facilities; poor capacity utilization; insecurity; and, inadequate skills.

The Cluster Concept was argued, to create a community of businesses located together in which members would seek enhanced environmental, social and corporate performance towards effective global trade competitiveness. It would enable government to concentrate infrastructure and other amenities necessary for the smooth operation of businesses in identified locations. Clustering would also permit greater focusing of public resources as infra-structural facilities would be concentrated in identified locations especially for industrial and commercial purposes.

Moreover, as has been noted, because of geographic proximity of firms as well as financial and other business institutions, clus-tering would enhance the effectiveness of the innovation pro-cess necessary to kick start Nigerian industrial take-off. It would also encourage localization economies and enhance the likelihood of inter-firm technology and information transfers; and, equally motivate Nigerian companies to go into product specialization and adoption of new technologies.

According to the policy, the Cluster Concept would operate on five platforms: Free Trade Zones; Industrial Parks; Industrial Clusters; Enterprise Zones; and, Incubators. It defined Free Trade Zones, as oases of economic activities usually situated in the proximity of seaports or international airports (entry and exit points). In such zones, goods are brought in or taken out of the country without being subjected to the usual duties, since it is considered to be outside custom's territory. Government would therefore establish more of such zones across the country to complement existing ones, while the zones would grant special incentives to attract For-eign Direct Investments (FDI).

Industrial parks were explained as mega parks covering areas of not less than 30 —50 square kilometres for large manufacturing companies with high value addition in the production of finished products. The plan according to the policy is to locate at least one park in each of the six geo-political zones, with such parks focus-ing on processing products, in which the zones had both compara-tive and competitive advantages.

Furthermore, it defined Industrial Clusters as oases of industrial activities and commerce, covering areas between 100 and 1,000 hectares, which would be controlled by the organized private sector. Usually smaller in scope than the parks, these clusters were to be established by the states and local governments. Enterprise Zones according to the policy are platforms of 5 —30 hectares, targeted at scaling up businesses from the informal sector to the formal sector. The aim, is to tackle some of their problems, which ranged from skills deficiency, funding, access to credit to infrastructure. The target was to locate at least one of these specialized zones in every state capital, local government and major cities. The last leg of the Cluster Concept are the Incubators, which were described as start-up centres for new and inexperienced entrepreneurs, such as graduates of tertiary institutions, investors and vocational persons wishing to set up their own businesses. In these centres, prospective start-up companies would be equipped with entrepreneurial skills and programs aimed at nurturing them from scratch to maturity. These incubators would be attached to higher institutions and research institutes.

CHAPTER 2

Generation Of Economic Stimuli

Stimuli are essential in the dynamics of economic development. They propel speedy growth of economic indices. Proofs of stimuli in the economy, which abound in the enriched discipline of quantum economics, are high velocity of commercial activities, and the viability of these stimuli is evidenced by tangible results in the form of economic expansion. Again, what is most visible in the situations described are increased demand of products and increased income leading to increased savings.

Two essential facts have been raised in the foregoing scenarios, increased output and increased rate of savings. The existence of these economic indicators suggest increased rate of growth in the economy, which are largely occasioned by growth stimuli in the system. Incidentally, fast-moving commodities are excellent examples of stimuli.

According to Harrod-Domar Model, high saving rates and high output lead to increased rate of economic growth. This postulation was independently developed by British economist, Sir Roy F. Harrod and Russian-American economist, Evsey D. Domar, in 1939 and 1946 respectively.

This theory of economic growth in its simplified version, states that the rate of growth of the Gross National Product (GNP) is determined jointly by the savings ratio and the capital-output ratio. In other words, the rate of growth of an economy, that is, change in Y over Y, is dictated by the incremental rate of savings (s) and diminutive rate of capital formation (k). A robust and rapidly growing savings and output translate to accelerated economic growth of a state. This model was a precursor of exogenous model of economic growth.

Against this backdrop, the opportunities MSMEs create and motivate expansion of income, level of savings and output which translate to economic growth are practically enormous. Equally, the tenacious spirit of entrepreneurs, who are MSMEs players, will be optimally charged to action in response to the stimulated business environment created by this industrial whirlwind. Our producers and craftsmen will step up standard of their products in healthy competition with the world class benchmark. It is needless to say that within this stimulation of industrial landscape the manufacturing sector will be receiving magnificent boosts. The logic is simple. Nigeria being a huge market, improving the effective demands of citizens will amazingly have effect on the total revenue (and hopefully profit maximization: when marginal revenue equates marginal cost) of producers and manufacturers. It is noteworthy that poor product standards, leading to price elasticity of demand equating to zero, on commodities, is disastrous. This is because preference to imported goods will plummet the exchange rate of our currency, deepening the economic doldrums.

Nigerian economy requires effective diversification of its economic base. So much so now that the country is facing nose-dive movement in the revenue from the oil sector which should necessitate energy meant to form the bulwark for wealth creation. Again, the potentials for diversification of the economy mainly lie in the domains of manufacturing, agricultural, solid mineral, tourism and the service sectors. Value chain enterprises promote the activities of these sectors. Therefore, value chain enterprises will adequately contribute to the transformation of the nation's economy.

The dual sector economic model of Professor William Arthur Lewis postulates the harnessing of abundant human resources for industrial development. Because it has been demonstrated that the private sector is disposed enough to employ more labour than the government would, the Lewis model tacitly therefore lends credence to private sector driven economy. On this strength governments should not hesitate in commencing journey of transforming their areas. Their economic trajectory should centre on wealth creation and wealth creation is the domain of the private sector. Farmers in the rural areas, shoe producers in market sheds, carpenters, entrepreneurs and investors in the urban areas constitute the private sector. They are good at driving the economy to prosperity. What they require from the government is enabling environment and prime to that is atmosphere that adequately rewards their efforts.

Government provides good economic landscape where abundant human resources will be galvanized for maximization of production. The return on investment will be divested in other areas of the economy for infrastructural development, consequently. It is important to bring to the fore that Micro, small and Medium-Scale Enterprises (MSMEs), which are part of privately owned businesses, blossom in an environment where due process is paramount. The due process is an effective economic 'seedlings' for industrial transformation.

The agricultural resource is also a wealth mine. There are various and different agricultural reserves. Effective promotion of agribusiness and perfection of supply chain mechanisms make farming attractive. This is aimed at adding value at every point of the process line, thereby making the profession lucrative. The expansion of the access to financial service, and summing them up to private-sector driven approach is vital to enable its sustenance and effective value addition. Value chain management is at the core of the attainment of the new prosperous society. The development of industries is essentially vital for employment creation, tourism development, improved IGR and maximization of resource potentialities. Education is a key to development of nations. Capacity building to address skills gap in work places in the government and for the private sector is essential. Tertiary education opportunities should be widened thorough establishment of such institutions which are geared towards technological enhancements.

The mentioned sectors have the potentialities for increased benefits, but it is important that the private sector is at the fulcrum of this revival. The Civil Societies have been pivotal for social work and volunteerism which focuses on various clusters covering areas of health, community development, child development, water and sanitation, malaria and constructions. World Bank and African Development Bank have emerged as firm partners for Nigeria's development. They have assisted the country to develop various sectors of the government. Of course, effectively, other development partners have policies that will rub off well for speedy economic development of the economy.

MSMEs are pivotal for economic growth, therefore are essential for the transformation of any society. They account for over 50 per cent of GDPs in the developing economies and participate in every sector. Their contributions to the economy include accelerated industrialization, employment generation, curbing of rural-urban drift and diversification of the revenue base of the government. They are also sources of innovations and entrepreneurships. The growth of these enterprises is largely dependent on the enabling environment provided by governments. As such, governments at all levels strive to provide the desired environment for MSMEs to thrive because the development of their domains is predicated upon the successes of those enterprises. Suffice it to say that people-oriented governments desire to achieve economic development because its outcomes are improved standard of living for the people.

The developmental trajectory of Abia State Government has galvanized enabling environment for the growth of the micro, small and medium scale enterprises. The hallmark which has been efficient infrastructural provisions and people-oriented policies has provided enabling environment for enterprises to thrive. The rural electrification, skill acquisition programmes, favourable policy formulations, road constructions and market development in the urban and rural areas are proofs of the government's penchant for effective incubation and flourishing of MSMEs in the state.

The concept of business with profit-orientation in recent times is finding relevance in the government circles as evidenced by the urgency with which commercialisations of corporations are being undertaken. The traditional method of governance that embodies social interventions for the citizen's wellbeing has not given way to full optimisation of peoples potentials through "enterprisation" of the government sector. This has been the bane of the so called Third World countries. The indicator of depletion of the size of Third World Countries explains itself as to the effect of change management. This change management is anchored on turning around the workings of the government from that marked by pettiness in government, to the type characterised by business in government. Hitherto, governments had not aligned to the current trajectories that have enriched the developed countries. There have been wonderings why private companies thrive while state owned corporations do not stand the test of time or sustain reasonable trend of prosperity. As the free market economic system has in its merits, healthy competitions and free participation, which beam a search light on business, there should be no exception in the entire sectors of the system, including the government sector. There is no economic system that abhors business enterprise, but what seem to be observed in the concept of communism is detest of exploitation; and then market forces almost wards off exploitation, using the invisible hand as penned by Adam Smith. Entrepreneurship is what should be encouraged in the economic systems. And as they are co-opted, government sector should not be left out. When government makes profits, reasonably, it boasts the services rendered to the people. Therefore, there is need to refocus the tenets of government to be business-oriented, and this will positively rub off on various facets of the government that have been dormant for some time.

It only requires a paradigm shift, a change of mind-set and orientation. There are businesses, especially, the private sector experiencing magnanimous transformation within the confines of the state. Why the whole should then cannot be prosperous? The answer is in refocusing the direction of governance, or strengthening its focus if its original direction is ideal. But if it requires refocusing; then to where? The question which this book you are holding attempts to address. Focusing has been noted to be of immense importance. Eagle, whose power of focus has remained classical in the conceptualization of special sight possessions, is a case in point. In the foreword of their book, The Power of Focus, Canfield, Hansen and Hewitt noted that "the main reason most people struggle professionally and personally is simply lack of focus. They procrastinate or allow themselves to be easily distracted and interrupted". They insisted that purposeful life and indeed, government is "not hocus-pocus, it's all about focus".

The celebrated Acemoglu and Robinson's Why Nations Fail posited and rightly too that inclusive economic and political institutions existent in nations are reasons for their prosperity. Similarly, the extractive economic and political institutions in nations place down in poverty situation that they find themselves. This boils down to the sensibilities and competence of individual government in view of the welfare of the governed. The importance of the government in determining the fate of its citizens is again brought to the fore. They are saddled with the responsibilities of charting the course of the nation to prosperity.

Nigeria as a democratic nation and to foster this statute, government has three organs and three tiers. The executive, legislature and judiciary are the three organs, while the first tier (exclusive list), the second tier (the concurrent list) and the third tier (the residual list). Nigeria operates a mixed economic system where capitalism is fortified with government interventions. These are to streamline government targets in order for them to be met. The targets are challenging, some particularly so. But if the right policies are put in place, nationally, we believe that they are achievable. Progress is dependent on national governments in all countries strengthening their commitment to poverty reduction.

Internationally, in the last few decades, there has been enormous progress in development. Since the 1960s, life expectancy in developing countries has risen from 46 to 64 years, infant mortality rates have halved, there has been an increase of more than 80 per cent in the proportion of children enrolled in primary school, and there has been a doubling of access to safe drinking water and basic sanitation.

Over this period, we have learned a lot about what works in development - and about what does not. Our task is to apply these lessons on a larger scale in the context of globalisation. It is clear that development strategies must be adapted to local circumstances and must be nationally owned and nationally led by developing and transition countries. But it is the belief that globalisation creates unprecedented new opportunities for sustainable development and poverty reduction, and for progress against the targets.

Effective governments and efficient markets are both essential if developing countries are to reap the benefits of globalisation and to make that process work for poor people. While the market fundamentalism of the 1980s and early 1990s has been thoroughly discredited, it is now almost universally accepted that efficient markets are indispensable for effective development. But equally important are effective governments - which are both competent in carrying out their basic functions, and more accountable, responsive and democratic, with a bigger voice for poor people in the determination of government policy.

Globalisation gives added urgency to the task of strengthening government systems in developing countries. Private capital is highly mobile and will go to where business can be carried out safely and where it can make the best return. Weak and ineffective states, with problems of corruption, inadequate infrastructure and cumbersome bureaucratic procedures, are not an attractive destination for these flows.

In contrast, those countries that apply rules and policies predictably, ensure law and order, invest in human capital (particularly education and health) and protect property rights, are likely to attract higher levels of inward investment and trade and to generate faster economic growth. A key function of governments is the provision of law and order. And this is also a priority for the poor. One of the findings of the World Bank's Voices of the Poor report was that poor people attach enormous importance to security - security from violence and security for their property. Without this, they find it impossible to improve their lives. The poor worldwide also tend to be very distrustful of existing police and criminal justice systems. Far from protecting people from violence, too often elements within the police and justice systems are themselves sources of violence and abuse.

CHAPTER 3

The Significance Of Education And Communication

Education is the key, goes the age-long adage. The level of literacy in a place determines the degree of development and civilization in that area. In other words, improved civilization correlates positively with expansion of education in a society. Of course, education goes beyond the four walls of classrooms and colleges. Reading this book, for example, provides enlightenment and education for the reader, albeit the art of reading finds foundation in formal education. Also, informal and non-formal means of imparting knowledge to people are found in the homes, workplaces and worship centres. Walking around the arts exhibition rooms and beholding the artefacts also affords a new knowledge to the tourists. Equally, travels and social networking are avenues knowledge is passed from one to another, which adds value to the life of the leaner. Education provides sensitization and awareness.

In the light of the above, adequate sensitization and awareness creation on vital issues regarding MSMEs are critical to the development of the sub-sector. The information age is around the corner and it is characterized by efficiency and value-addition in day-to-day activities, higher productivity in industries and excellent deliveries in the service sector. The MSMEs must plug into this opportunity for maximum contribution of this sub-sector to nation building. Similarly, stakeholders in the MSMEs should take advantage of the information age and utilize relevant data to enhance research & development in the sub-sector.

E-library and other media complexes, therefore, must be geared towards redefining the information reproduction, storage and retrieval systems of the society, bringing to bear the educational and cultural uniqueness of the economy, with emphasis on its industrial cluster development. This information and communication materials centre will reposition the economy's education nucleus. The architecture of education and communication must therefore epitomise government's amenability to technological revolution.

The Abia State government has plugged education and communication into the MSMEs development. The regime of information technology simply warns that those who do not join now will lose the early benefits, and definitely must be compelled to tag along. Just like computers phased out typewriters, and the invention of the printing press by Johannes Gutenberg in the 15th century revolutionised the information and communication technology.

Quick access to information is indispensable for real-time research information for product modification and styling. The workstations should have the capacity to feed the cluster sites and institutions within the state and beyond with no limitations. Equally, media houses will plug into this digital reservoir for information and archival materials.

Rural networking is another important aspect of communication and education. Communication revolution will spark rural networking. Rural communities will thereby hook to the networks. By so doing the cultural heritage of the people will be preserved, energized and mend into the MSMEs transformation for increased results.

Indeed, the increased result is assured because our culture melts into the way we do things, including agriculture, architecture, social security and hospitality. These will be expanded with the operation of the e-library. The world is evolving speedily, the practise of e-learning and e-research is plugged into the e-library system. Needless to say that digital library defies the constraints of space, time and distance. The library which operates round the clock has materials which can be accessed from any distance, regardless of number of users per time.

Again, in compliance with government policies, such as the cashless regime, will be kindled, due to acclimatization through constant use of the system. It is pertinent to note that most institutions and corporations hire or conduct examinations electronically. Abia State is amenable to this trend as evidenced by distribution of computer sets to students in the state school system by the state government. Also, e-journals have emerged as fulcrum of journalism and research efforts. This emergence has increased knowledge which has been likened to the renaissance of 14th to 17th century that metamorphosed to industrial revolution in the western world.

Renaissance is sine qua non for cultural movement; hence the IT revolution sparks renewed cultural development for advancement and growth. Culture is described as values, attitudes, beliefs, and assumptions people share about themselves and others, and about the world in which they live. It includes the institutions, customs and communication patterns people have created to meet their needs. The norms and customs of the people have endured over the years; these comprise material and non-material forms of culture. The agricultural and architectural practices, for example, reserve cherished affinity with the cultural practices of the people. The e-library transforms these rich potentials for maximum prosperity for the people. The e-library will anchor in the huge cultural reserves to optimize its successes, knowing full well that IT renaissance is pivotal in excellence in arts, technology, agriculture, science, literature, music, technocracy, architecture and handicrafts. The renewed dexterity in sporting activities and rarefied show of hospitality will receive additional impetus through e-library, which will also develop the contemporary arts and tourism potentials.

CHAPTER 4

Mid Term Review [Mtr]

Midterm Review (MTR) has been the domain of multilateral development banks, such as World Bank and African Development Bank (AfDB). However, it is not exclusive property of these entities. Governments, realising the effectiveness, sustainability and scalability of this approach, can adopt and adapt same. Midterm review has concise objective, which is to take stock of business to be able to chart ways forward. It is a development term used to describe a comprehensive assessment of implementation of plans or projects vis-à-vis its objective. It is an action for soul-searching. MTR requires participation of entire stakeholders for productive brainstorming. The brainstorming is coordinated based on specialization so as to obtain good results from each grouping.

More than other merits, MTR summits thicken the bonds that hold together each human resource elements in the organization. It is not the mere convening of the meeting that does the magic, rather the sum total of both formal and informal activities that take place. The brainstorming, experience-sharing, disagreeing-to-agree, and divergent-opinion-championing, etcetera set the stage and make the meeting worth its bidding. At this point, the organization as a corporate entity is reinforced. Corporate organization in its real sense of the term is likened to Superorganismic arrangement. Paul Herr, in his book, Primal Management: Unravelling the Secrets of Human Nature to Drive High Performance, noted that "(i)n biology, Superorganism is a group of individual organism that act as one- like a colony of army ants. Ant colonies, working as coordinated units, can defeat creature hundreds of times their size". He went ahead to state that "(h)uman beings possess a sophisticated form of social bonding that some psychiatrists refer to as Cathexis. This social bonding mechanism underlie relationships of all types, and corporation, unfortunately, are not aware of it". In a conventional MTR meeting, every stakeholder is required as his contribution is critical to the coveted mission that birthed the organization or project.

Stock-taking being the thrust of the MTR examines the achievement, prospects and challenges faced in pursuing the goals set out at the outset by organizations, programmes and projects. By implication, re-visitation of visions, goals, missions, objectives and plans (works, procurement, and disbursement etcetera) underlie an effective MTR. Vision is a conceived desired state of the future while mission is a path to reach that destination. Strategies are adopted means to move along the mission (path) to the vision. Goals are high frequency milestones along the way to attaining our vision while objectives are low frequency milestones meant to enhance the achievement of the goals. Plans are short-time details to achieve set out objectives. Thus we have work plans, procurement plans and disbursement plans.

Procurement plan is a framework for procurement outcomes. Work plan and budget are the bases for procurement and disbursement plans. Procurement plan describes the process, procedures, timing, estimates and deliverables expected from procurement activities. In recent times, the World Bank has added the adjective 'result-based' on the term procurement planning, connoting the urge for impact of this plans on the system. In other words, procurement planning should not be for the fun of it but to produce tangible results, especially as it relates to the developing world to justify the effort expended, and to be true to the vision of the World Bank.

As noted, three major aspects of the organization are x-rayed in detail during MTRs, namely; achievement, prospects and challenges. Organizational achievement is viewed from the standpoint of the output and outcome. Outputs are the structures while the outcomes are the effects. School block, for instance, is the output while increased students' enrolment and literacy rates are respectively the short- and long-term outcomes.

The project achievement will really base on the objective upon which they are embarked. There is a satisfactory achievement when objective within the term states that 40 school blocks and 35 school blocks were constructed. However, the foregoing is case to the contrary when the objective is to increase students enrolment by 60% while the 40 blocks erected were empty within the period reviewed. Most World Bank projects emphasize outcomes as opposed to output, without prejudice to the fact that output is precursor to effective outcome.

Organizational prospects define their tangible potentials for growth and stability. Given the reality of socioe-conomic and environmental dynamics, potentials non-existent at the inception of the programme or by one reason or the other, will be taken into consideration at the present review. New policies, plans, programmes, projects, personalities and people will be co-opted to positively impact on the program for which review is undertaken.

Challenges are inevitable hence it will be thoroughly analysed to forestall or cushion their influence on the programme. When challenges are identified and addressed, renewed stability and accelerated growth are experienced in programmes. If anything, challenges are critical because they jumpstart innovations and new thinking. Usually challenges of resource deficient cap this aspect of project review. The resources include money, material and manpower. Primal being money because it can virtually procure the other two resources. Conducive environment (political, geographical and economic) is also essential for successful operation of organizations but that is assumed out of the purview of MTR but institutional. It is a little ambiguous here but the point being made is if the state does not exist, then there is no basis for MTR. Again, the economic environment is not isolated but global, as such, outside the control of the mechanizations of the organization.

Mid-term review is amenable to critical sectors hence the inexorableness of bringing to focus the quadruplet of environment, agriculture, water and poverty issues. They are wedded together and have severally and particularly been topical in recent times. Poverty is a common multiple of agriculture, environment, and water. They are so interconnected that default of each affects others adversely. Poor water availability is attributed to climate change whose major culprit is unhealthy agricultural practice. It has been forecasted that poverty will be a thing of the past in future. But it is not until technology has made good the rich dreams which it had brandished. Technology is expecting agriculture to be practiced with least adverse impact on the environment (with abundant food supply), water recycling will ensure water sufficiency and environmental degradation will abate, as a result.

X-raying environment, multilateral development banks, particularly World Bank, are interested in environmental issues. The latter has recently published a broadened environmental and social framework, to replace a couple of narrowing operational policies (OPs) and Bank's Procedures (BPs) to guide on environmental (and social) practices and mechanisms. In the foregoing, the rhetoric suggests that robust economy is underpinned by sound environment, productive agriculture and water resources.

On water, its essence is aptly demonstrated in the award winning

Rango, Gore Verbinski's 2011 American 3D computer-animated action comedy film, where the fate and existence of a populace are determined and manipulated by artificial scarcity of water orchestrated by the town mayor. Water is of topmost essence in the daily existence and activities of men, animal and plants. United Nations General Assembly Resolution 64/292 declared water human rights which call for governments' policies to ensure adequate and affordable quantities of safe water for domestic use.

Statistics show that water demand will increase by 30-50% by 2050 (considering that by that year, global population is projected to attain 9 billion mark) owing largely to population growth, rising consumption, urbanization and energy needs. Therefore, countries that are already facing population crisis coupled with climate change and degraded watersheds are already in excruciating situation and unpredictably gloomy future.

In his inspiring TED talk captioned, '4 Ways we can avoid a catastrophic Drought', David Sedlak outlined the ways to ensure a watered life to include; Storm and rain water-harvesting, Water Reuse, Water Conservation, and Seawater desalination. In his didactic lecture, he convincingly argued that water harvest following rainfall will be helpful after such have been treated and purified. He also submitted that water recycling achieved through treatment mechanisms returns to water elements to hygienically acceptable state. However, much as he included Seawater desalination as a choice, he noted that this is energy intensive and somewhere not environmentally friendly.

Until the above and related initiatives are implemented, already, 50% of global population are already facing severe water deficit. This has been attributed to glamour for uncontrolled food production achieved this period. Whereas this feat is commendably achieved, it however distorted the global water configuration. The food production pursuit has thus caused expansion of farmlands known as 'extensification' into the wild reservation, distorting the ecosystem, expanded irrigation schemes, and water contamination through excessive fertilization application. Water variability is also a challenge in its own merit. It is noted that 25 per cent of the world population has endured abnormal rainfall episode twice in a year, as opposed to rarity of such incidents. There could be rain shocks or unprecedented dryness that are ordinarily expected to happen once in a century are now of frequent occurrence.

The Paradox of Value exemplified by the use of diamond and water commodities by Adam Smith in the 16th century remained centre of debate, even to this day. The poser argues on the apparent contradiction on the values of the commodities as expressed by their prices which runs contrary to their usefulness. But due to the global high scarcity of water, the import of the poser may be changing. Climate change conundrum has distorted rains pattern which introduces drought to the area where it was a stranger; and similarly, heavy rainfall to the area where it was least expected

On poverty, in the foregoing had been defined as a multivariate function. Almost every undesirable index positively correlates with it. Endangered, drought, and hunger orbit the forces of poverty. Ending poverty is fittingly first in the list of Sustainable Development Goals (SDGs). Now, most development agencies have poverty reduction as their chief targets. Poverty is hinged on vicious cycle. The critical concern poverty wields in the society makes building synergy to fight it very strategic. The Community Driven Development (CDD) cannot be overlooked, therefore, because there is growing need to break its cycle with innovative approaches.

The approach of CDD, as a mechanism for poverty reduction and local development, has emerged and grown rapidly since the mid-1990s with the support of funding agencies, particularly the World Bank. The approach gives community groups control over decision making and the use of block grant resources for grass-roots development. CDD's distinguishing feature is community control of resources. In CDD programs, communities are active participants who prioritize their development needs and compete for resources by expressing interests for available and benefitting assistance.

CDD has been attracting attention because, when properly implemented, it is more developmentally effective than other approaches. Evidence also indicates that CDD is likely to offer better performance in cost recovery and the operation and maintenance of the selected infrastructure and services due to a strong sense of ownership of the community members. CDD can demonstrably operate to scale and is relevant across the sectors. Although great potential has been demonstrated in the provision of "goods and services that are small in scale and not complex, and that require local co-operation.

CDD is not just developmentally effective at the activity level; It also aligns well with some of the higher level strategic directions of organizations. Properly designed, CDD has much to offer in terms of the overarching poverty reduction agenda and achieving both income and non-income millennium development goals. It promotes inclusive patterns of growth and civil society demand for

good local governance, while offering opportunities for better results in priority sectors such as rural and urban infrastructure.

CDD has become a popular development intervention because of its approach toward empowering local decision-making and its reputation for getting resources to communities efficiently. The approach departs from traditional approaches to development by enabling communities and local institutionsthan central governmentstake the lead in identifying and managing community level investments. The World Bank currently supports approximately 400 CDD projects in 94 countries valued at almost $30 billion.

Over the past 10 years, CDD investments have represented between 5 and 10 per cent of the overall World Bank lending portfolio.

However, CDD is not applicable to all development programs. There are also risks and limitations with it. Success requires a significant level of capacity development assistance to community members or groups, local governments, and other implementers, which may mean a longer preparation period when first implemented.

Close supervision is required during its implementation. Challenges typical to traditional development projects may still need to be managed well, such as problems of elite capture, limitations in inclusiveness, technical suitability of certain infrastructure choices, adverse spill-over effects of certain infrastructure decisions on neighbouring communities, and long-term sustainability. In addition, CDD-induced governance and fund transfer structures should eventually be integrated into decentralized local governance and budgeting systems once community participation becomes a routine.

CHAPTER 5

Due Process

The term Due Process has effectively stuck into the lexicon of Nigerian State and indeed has become a household name since the turn of the century. It is the systematic and keen observance of best practices in the execution of disbursement and procurement actions. Due process underlies fairness, economy, efficiency, transparency, competition, openness and profitability and Productivity. These are expatiated below.

Fairness: Fairness exists when there is a balancing out of preferences. In other words, the preference is spread across the spectrum of interest expressers, in such a way that none is particularly prefers to others. Objectivity is the watchword.

Economy: Economy is effectively having value for money. In array of choices, the one that offers most with less cost is desirable. This is done in full consideration of other factors both in the short and long run.

Efficiency: This involves timely delivery and achieving less with more, also lending credence to the overall pursuit in procurement of having value for money. Efficiency also connotes producing with less waste proportion. Higher efficiency is achieved when aggregate input is fully translated and responsible to the outcome of an activity.

Transparency: When you drop an object in a transparent glass, people from every side see it. More so, when something is performed in the full glare of every eye, it will be transparent to all and sundry. So, the terminology of transparency needs not much narrative. Everything at every point in an activity that is performed in stages of procurement process must be open and understood by everyone. Nothing is hidden. There will be 360-degree opportunity for siting. Once more, like an object in a plain glass cup, it is left crystal clear.

Competition: Competition involves two or more persons given equal opportunities to achieve a goal where there will be emergence of a winner. Competition is a fulcrum of lowest price offers at the right quality. With competition in perspective, and the bidders pre-informed about this scenario, there is every tendency that each bidder will beat down their prices. This is simply rational. Every supplier wants to sell and they will achieve that by quoting the lowest prices through marking up by the lowest margin.

Openness: Openness is like transparency, but with the addition of the allowance to probe further and given the chances of inquiry and questionings. Persons should be clarified on what they missed to understand. Openness is better practiced with high level pro-activity, in assuming what could attract people's attention and explaining it before the suspicion.

Profitability: While some procurements target social services, others are meant for economic and income generation. In this regard, items are procured with the view to achieving profitability. In this case, its value for money principle will be measured by the profit margin attained. If farm produce, for example, are provided for beneficiaries to add value and sale to make profit, attention should thus be paid on the cost of the inputs, vis-à-vis the market price of those final products. The profit margin should attain such a level as to cover the value addition element. The FADAMA Project is a good example whereby the Project Development Objective (PDO) is CDD (economic). Profit in social aspects may not be easily measurable directly, in monetary terms. But the impact is visible.

Productivity: Productivity beams on volume of output with respect to resource input. Procurement framework is expected to engender high productivity. Items produced are hoped to enhance increased production with very minimal input. The ICT Systems procured are meant to facilitate high speed production of document, in contrast with the former system that constituted a setback to official production; so also with mobility and infrastructural equipment. Technically, since procurement advocates value for money mantra; productivity clearly follows because when the output is kept constant and input is decreased, the result is promotion of high productivity.

Procurement entities or regulatory bodies on procurement keep unit price databanks. This assists procurement units to manage estimates in the procurement plans and crosscheck quotations of bidders, especially on non-competitive methods such as direct purchases. In the projects, such as Community and Social Development Project (World Bank assisted), which uses CDD approach; unit price database is maintained based on LGAs basis to enable adequate supervision of benefitting communities on procurement aspects.

Procurement practice is essentially developed by the group of Multilateral Development Banks (MDBs), International Financing Institutions (IFIs), governments, organised corporate institutions and the civil society from the spectrum of due process, in order to achieve the common objective of sustainable development, especially in the developing countries. Ever since, procurement has become an embodiment of dynamism, where no single year passed without a modification and advancement in at least a rule of procedure of procurement of any development agency. The group of MDBs and IFIs includes, World Bank, African Development Banks, Asian Development Banks, Inter-American Development Bank, European Investment Bank, European Bank for Reconstruction and Development, Development Bank of Latin America, Asia Infrastructure Investment Bank, amongst others.

And the governments include Nigeria, Ghana, Sierra Leone, Uganda, Indonesia, and Myanmar, just to mention but a few. Come to think of it, the Country Procurement Assessment Review (CPAR) conducted in 2000, for example, made Nigeria a partner in the development of international standards in due process following their embrace of the investigation, in which the government fully partook.

Procurement covers an arc on the circumference of supply-chain mechanism. Whereas supply-chain is a whole gamut of process from production to distribution, procurement carters for logistical and supply aspects of the cycle. Procurement is the acquisition of goods, works, consulting and non-consulting services at the right quality and quantity, for project implementation obtained at the lowest cost of ownership. The lowest cost of ownership points to the fact that obtaining value for money, which is paramount, hinged on due process where transparency is key.

Modern procurement is relatively new globally, and essentially so in African continent. It is multi-sectoral and cuts across diverse disciplines. In recent past, procurement was seen as automatic and as such, an objective approach; but following failures of contracts, elements of subjectivity has been advised because success of contract management is vital in procurement procedure. In an award of contract, the most advantageous bid is now preferred because it has fulfilled the qualification criteria, been substantially responsiveness and lowest evaluated cost. This is essential to ensure contract implementation successes.

An important milestone in procurement sub-sector in Nigeria was the assenting of the Public Procurement Act into Law in 2007. Several states have also followed suit in cascading and domesticating that act into their law by State Houses of Assembly.

As noted, procurement has gained popularity recently. The public and the private sectors are experiencing the wind of change, although there are slight variations both in application and momentum of embrace. Public procurement, which is applicable in the public sector, has come to stay as an epicentre for effective due process. This paradigm, which has become the fulcrum of good governance across the horizons of governments globally, seeks to reduce corruption and its companions.

The five procurement rights are expatiated below;

Right Quality: Effective procurement requires that supplies meet standards specified. In fact, it is conventional that deliveries must be the highest standard available in the market. This does not matter whether the procurer knows about it or not. In motor vehicles, for instance, the latest model is expected to be supplied. If a bidder quotes for 2016 model of a vehicle, for instance, and as he is about to supply, 2017 model surfaces in the market, the bidder is liable to supply the latter. Again, it must meet the demands of state's regulatory bodies. Examples of regulatory agencies in Nigeria include; National Agency for Food and Drug Administration and Control (NAFDAC), Standards Organization of Nigeria (SON), Consumer Protection Commission (CPC), amongst others. It is basic that product supplied must comply with the clauses of guidelines of these regulatory organizations.

Right Quantity: The right quantity proviso must be met, equally. Procurement officers must be alive to their responsibilities at this point. Some items come in cards, placed in packs and packed in cartons. The completeness of these supplies must be verified thoroughly. The stores and inventory system must be functioning effectively to give accurate information about the quantity to requisition for, at each procurement action. The knowledge and practice of sound inventory system is vital in this circumstance. This equips the procurement officer during the preparation of procurement plan. Of course, this knowledge is generated with the interface of other departments to be able collate their various departmental needs.

Right Price: Prices of items must be right. Thus, they must be verified and confirmed to congruent what the market sells. This is achieved by establishing unit price database through market researches. And by this, procurement officers will be abreast with the mark-ups of suppliers. As such, the incidence of collusion will easily be detected by these practice, especially in less competitive procurement methods.

Knowledge of prices assists procurement practitioners in preparation of procurement plans. These are provided as

estimated, which are of utmost importance considering that it serves as good compass for effective and result-based procurement. It should be borne in mind that in theory of demand in economics, price is a function of quantity. Therefore, price determines quantity and in that way, will be measured by the quantity of items it commands.

Right Time: Time is of utmost essence in procurement. Items must be supplied when needed to avert gap in operations and usage. At lager scale, seasons could be the consideration, and then proper targeting should be the guiding principle to engage a consultant or contractor at the right season. Some, assignments are in segments, some activities must be completed before next actions, therefore, effort must be made to ensure that rights schedules are adhered to. Again, the stores must be functioning effectively to give accurate information about the time to requisition. Therefore the capacity of the stores officer must be built for proper application of store techniques.

Right Place: This is at the core of procurement especially in large supplies. Logistics and transport are critical at this point. Supplier must be done at the most appropriate and convenient place. It will be double assignments, and often, burdening to delivered good at inappropriate places. It is essential that huge haulages are targeted at the proper locations once and for all. The knowledge of Incoterms is necessary at this point especially for large procurement. More necessary is when the supplies may involve importations, especially in the case of International Competitive Bidding (ICB).

Right place also relates to the safe-keeping of items procured. In communities that engage in the implementation of their felt-need projects, items procured for micro-project implementation must be stored appropriately safe from theft and harsh weather conditions.

As noted in the foregoing, failure of a single 'right' will retard the entire process. Taking 'right quality' for instance; if a sub-standard item is supplied, there will be call for re-supply, this will over-stretch the time for implementation and the objective of the project will have been missed.

There are five major categories of procurement for the purpose of this book: they include Goods, Civil Works, Non-Consulting Services, Consultancy and Community Contracting. Within these categories are methods of processing them. These vary amongst agencies and countries, but generally, under works, goods and non-consulting services, which share same methods, we have

International Competitive Bidding (ICB), Limited International Bidding (LIB), National Competitive Bidding (NCB), National Shopping (NS), Framework Agreement (FA), Force Account, and Direct Contracting (DC). Under Consultancy, there are two major sides; namely, where price is not a factor and where price is a factor. There are also two major classifications; namely, firm-based consultancy and individual consultancy. Firm-based is identified by its legal status, such as organizational registration while individual consultancy is identified by a professional personality. Threshold that attracts the former is higher and process more rigorous while the latter is associated with lesser threshold with less rigorous process and fewer procurement process for employment. Under firm based consultancy, we have methods such as QCBS, QBS, FBS, LCS, CQS, and SSS. These define the services category, which considers the usefulness of quality in the assignment being processed. Non-Consulting category sits at the borderline of goods, civil works and consultancy categories. It is an assignment where material equipment is intertwined with construction that demands special skill. Borehole construction is a good example.

Procurement plan is a framework for procurement outcomes. Procurement plan describes the process, procedures, timing, estimates and deliverables expected from procurement activities. In recent times, the World Bank has added the adjective 'result-based' on the term procurement planning, connoting the urge for impact of this plans on the system. In other words, procurement planning should not be for the fun of it but to produce tangible results, especially as it relates to the developing world to justify the effort expended, and to be true to the vision of the World Bank. This has been fruitfully emphasized during procurement planning clinics. Procurement planning clinics are conferences where procurement plans are drafted, supervised, produced and approved. This working together has the advantages of synergy building, planning within the confines of projections and review of other relevant procurement development. These reviews alongside other capacity building seminars afford satisfactory performances that lessen discomfitures during post procurement reviews.

Post procurement reviews are meant for cross-checking of procurement actions executed under post review procedures. Activities executed under prior review procedures receive step by step clearance thus do not require post review exercise. As already noted, procurement plan document contains such vital information as activity description, quantity, method and category of procurement, procedure of procurement, and estimated amounts. The timing component provides dates of period on which each procurement milestones is executed, ranging from preparation of bidding document and issuance to award and completion of contract. The accuracy of timeframe for each milestone is of utmost importance. Whereas the aforementioned forms the columns of the procurement plan table, there are two rows for each activity. The first captures the plan, while the other captures the actual. The plan row is populated before actions while the actual is filled after the actions.

Payment objectives are strict in most development agencies' projects, and most conscientiously, the World Bank and African Development Bank. The protocols are seriously observed to the extent that borrower are sanctioned for not meeting the obligation. Payment rules are provided in the contract form in the SBDs or IFQs. They are by extension, part of the Contract Agreement entered into during award of contract. There are different forms of agreement, according to agencies, but usually Lump Sum and Time-Based forms of agreement.

Payment periods are usually three weeks (21 days) after delivery. This is in the case of delivery of goods. Works or Consultancy categories may require payment in instalments. Conventionally, consultancy may have 3 to 4 payment stages and these follows completion of stages of works and submission of acceptable reports thereto (inception, interim, draft final, final) There could be a little deviations from the former in terms of timeframe for payment. In civil works, contractors are issued payment certificates at completion of milestones.

In some cases, suppliers may beat the period required to deliver. In such cases, suppliers are rewarded with bonuses if there is such clause in the Bidding Data Sheet. In the opposite, if the contractor excessed the time provided for delivery of assignment, liquidated damages will be charged on the vendor. The application of liquidated damages is usually the supplier pay the purchaser 5% of the total contract sum each working day that passes. At such a time 10% of the total contract sum is paid under the sanction, the contract is advised to be terminated.

Conventionally, payments are made after delivery for the case of goods. In the case of works or non-consulting category, there is usually are advance payment provision but such is supported by an Advance Payment Guarantee (APG). APGs are issued by Banks on behalf of the contractor covering amount paid in advance for work implementation to guarantee contractors due performance. The amount or portion of it is forfeited if the work is not executed as agreed. Performance Bond intends to confirm the contractor ability to execute the work awarded. This comes back-to-back to the Bid Security. At the award of contract, the bid securities of bidders are returned to the bidders, as the winner exchanges his with a Performance Bond.

CHAPTER 6

Project Appraisal Modalities

The preceding chapter took us on due process. And these entail being sufficiently systematic and taking cognizance of the established steps to achieve expected goals and objectives. The industrial cluster may be executed on the platform of project or programmes. Therefore, these suggest that at least there is a starting point and defined goals and objectives. By the foregoing, there should be determination for take-off. Hence, by definition, project appraisal is the assessment and ascertainment of readiness of the project implementation.

Merriam-Webster Dictionary defines appraise as "to evaluate the worth, significance of; especially, to give an expert judgement of the value or merit of". To attain a satisfactory mark, the project financial, monitoring, procurement and safeguard strategies must be placed on the get-go. Likewise during the MTR also already discussed earlier, stakeholders must undertake a mission to brainstorm and raise working documents that would come to be referred to as the Project Appraisal Document (PAD) and Project Implementation Manual (PIM).

Flagship programmes or projects such as industrial cluster for development of craftsmanship are taken seriously and feedback mechanism is fool proof to deliver to its mandate. Retroactive financing is considered at this point if multilateral funding is involved. Retroactive financing requires the purchasers to expend funds with the observance of due process, even though the execution of project is in view, and submit request for replenishment when disbursement commences.

The prime discussions which include financial, monitoring, procurement and safeguard strategies will be taken carefully.

Financial Strategies: The elements of financial management has budgeting at the helm, which include accounting and internal control. Under accounting we have funds flow and financial reporting while internal control has external audit.

Monitoring and Evaluation Strategies: Baseline models will have to be espoused with which to analyse and ascertain progress. These studies determine the enormity of the gap that existed pre-intervention. The tracking of output and outcomes are important to reflect on the project development objective. During the MTR, the adjusted indicators will be expedient given the realities on ground. Strategies for collection and collation of data for use is also of essence.

Procurement Strategies: Procurement is vital in programme and projects. Firstly, the procurement plan will have to be prepared and reviewed, in consonance with project development objective. The medium term plan is required during appraisal missions.

Safeguard Strategies: The safeguard is critical in project implementation for it to have developmental status. The

grievances, redress mechanism, is also pertinent looking from the point of view of social context, operating environment and safe guard risk.

Communication Strategies: This is critical in the success of every project. The beneficiaries, implementers, the funders and the initiators must be on the same page in the goings-on. The entire corpus of stakeholders must be carried along for smooth progress of the work and its sustainability. Also, in an event of conflict, the communication outfit steps in to bridge whatever communication gap that exists. A strategy therefore, must be developed to ensure enhanced productivity and efficiency.

The line of communication and report must also be established and recognized. The language and medium of communication must be identified and embraced, this is expedient because these must be in concordance with the norms and realities on ground.

CHAPTER 7

Holistic Transformation Through

INFRASTRUCTURAL DEVELOPMENT

Robust economy beckons on a country determined for holistic transformation. The entire sector-sparkplugs must be firing at full blast. The transportation, works, health, agriculture, commerce, trade and education must be steamed up. In the transportation sector, the air, land, sea and railways are excellent potentials. Taking railway for example, rail transportation facilitates movement of goods and individuals from one location to another by means of wheeled vehicle that run on rail tracks.

The contributions of rail systems to the growth of the sectors mentioned earlier are spectacular and cannot be over-emphasized. In retrospect, rail transportation during the colonial days was remarked as the colonialist's strategy in exploiting the cash crops and other valuables of the richly endowed colonies especially in Africa. Indeed, railway stimulates agriculture and trade because, it provides cheap means of movement of these goods from farm gates to the points they are needed, whether for onward shipment to importing countries or local production. This cycle adds value to the produce because it creates more demands of the raw materials. Of course, when values are added to a farm produce, encouragement is engendered in the agricultural practise, which reduces unemployment. Again, as the semi-finished or finished commodities are exported, foreign exchange is

earned, which bolsters the Gross Domestic Product [GDP]. Clearly, the economy is propelled to optimum comparative advantage in more trades with the revival of the railway lines.

Additionally, train transportation, at full operation, will save our roads from high rate of dilapidation when constructed or rehabilitated. The high decrepitude level is obviously partly as a result of undue pressure exerted on it, following high-tonnage haulage performed along the highways. By the incidence of reduced rate of road collapse, improved durability of asphalted roads will set in and will reduce government expenditure on roads maintenance, thereby, providing surplus to the budget.

As train transportation option is characterised by heavy-duty haulages and mass transportation, therefore, issues bordered on excessive fossil fuel emission, incessant high transport fares, bad road and its attendant problems, congested motor parks and airports will be addressed. The resultant effect is increased growth of the economy. In every ramification, the rail system is beneficial. With its nature of conveying large number of people to various destinations, rails development will practically cause a fewer vehicles to be on the road thereby reducing road accidents. Road accident in recent time has raised concerns due to high level of carnage it is associated with on our roads. These are other related occurrences adversely affect the developmental pursuit of government, hence, the pertinence to revive the safer alternative, of course, characterized by safety and cost-effectiveness.

Roads are paths to destinations. Therefore, they are essential infrastructure for human existence and accomplishment. Roads redefine the fortunes of people and have been proven as the major instrument for integration, explorations and economic progress. Testimonies abound as to the benefits that have been derived from these infrastructures. Typically, states in the developing countries, have more rural areas than urban areas, sufficing that the landscapes are more of rural settlements.

The rural roads have opened up the communities to market links for trade development, resulting to improved leeway for evacuation of farm produce and supply of farm inputs such as fertilizers, seedlings and farm tools. Developmental programmes and policies that target farm roads in the rural areas, have filliped economic development in those vicinities.

Rural road network stirs the evacuation of farm produce that guarantee good returns on investment. Indeed, the opportunity to evacuate farm produce elevates the profit margins of those products, owing to the propinquity to market places. Similarly, machineries are easily moved to farm areas, following accessibility of such locations by roads. Of course, these promotes full and semi-processing of farm yields to enable addition of value to such produce, thus an encouragement to rural farming. Rural farming reduces rural-urban drift and good road network in the communities have reduced drudgery of community members who are predominantly farmers. It is important to note that economic calculations are galvanized in such a way that the development of communities will improve livelihoods and increase productivity that support market development in the rural areas. This cycle is expected to reduce unemployment and favourably affect other macroeconomic indices.

The potentialities of an airport are broad. The markets that it will create will be enormous. In fact, the airport construction will come along with it an excellent comparative advantage given the multiplier effect its activities are going to generate. The airport project embarked by the state government is proudly people-oriented. It is important to note that aviation sector is identified as a heavy employer and major contributor to the GDP, principally, through taxes, jobs and supply-chain benefits. But beyond that, the 'catalyst' benefits through tourism, establishment of business cluster and connections between cities are effective variables for accelerated development.

CHAPTER 8

Social Development Through Non-Governmental Organizations

The concept of Non-Governmental Organization (NGO) has had a desirable connotation as an entity that embodies the role of complementing the effort of the government in her developmental endeavours. They are traditionally change agents and operate as not-for-profit organizations. The cardinal objective of every Non-Governmental Organization boils down to backstopping for the downtrodden and the less-privileged in caring and protection.

NGOs traditionally dwell on bringing succour to the less privileged. At a modest level, some assist less privileged individuals by providing them with cloths, shelter, food items and other basic materials for basic livelihood. They also undertake emergency responses, such as in the case of flood incidents and aiding victims of accidents to access first aid attention. Non-Governmental Organization NGOs assist in payment of medical bills of indigent individuals.

Further, depending on their thematic areas, some Non-Governmental Organization NGOs also intervene in psychosocial supports for the vulnerable groups, especially the terminally diseased, physically challenged, widowed and the aged. Non-Governmental Organization NGOs are also involved in research and development so as to keep abreast of the current issues and to pursue their profession in a systematic manner.

Beyond these, high profile Non-Governmental Organizations provide capital intensive empowerment facilities to the caregivers who are expected to extend necessary care and protection to the vulnerable, as a result of the instrumentalities of the empowerment they received. Empowerment describes the preparation of the poor to extricate from the chains of poverty into self-reliance and prosperity. Inclusive in the empowerment approach by NGOs are conditional cash transfer, skills acquisition training and provision of empowerment items. Clearly, founders of NGOs most often deny themselves comfort to cater for the needy. NGO work, indeed, is a calling that demands sacrifice.

Social work philosophies anchor in synergy-building and multiple-participation. This involves partnerships for solution provision. Partnerships are veritable tool for sustainable development. It is a tested and recognized instrument of economic transformation and improvement in the citizens' wellbeing. The expediency of this economic variable explains the evolvement of Private-Public Partnership (PPP) in the economic arsenal which has proved to be effective in poverty reduction, cooperate management and economic transformation.

In partnership, parties agree to cooperate in pursuit of mutual benefits. The "Iron sharpeneth iron" biblical injunction of the book of Proverbs summarizes the benefit of partnership. Increased investment in the form of financing and technical assistance is part of the gains by benefitting state. Of course, the by-products of synergy-building, which partnership creates, cannot be over-emphasized.

Interestingly, prime in the utilization of partnership as instrument for service delivery are development agencies. Development or donor agencies, either in the structure of bi-lateral, multilateral, Civil Society Organizations (CSOs), are established primarily to complement the effort of government in its developmental endeavours. They are usually not for profit, with major interest to better the lives of the downtrodden especially, in the developing countries.

The development agencies naturally align to the developmental pursuit of states and countries of focus to make relevant contribution, no gainsaying that the government is amenable to partnerships of these agencies as records clearly indicate.

The World Bank, African Development Bank, EU, UN, the USAID and other notable international NGOs such as the Cater Foundation, Bill and Melinda Gates Foundation, to mention but a few, have proved their mettle in the country through their contributions to nation building. In Abia State, indigenous NGOs and FBOs have also proved their resourcefulness as partners in progress in the state. They are actively involved in support for the economic development of the state.

World Bank portfolio is running in the economy and in tandem with the unprecedented support of the government has geared up its responses to various clusters of development. The World Bank has noted that the activities of development have contributed in reducing the poverty situation; this achievement is owing to the support of the government.

The list of benefits of development partnership has proved to be lengthy, but what is more important is for the two parties to take advantage of this mutual relationship to advance our frontiers towards the achievement of the transformation agenda, which dovetails into the SDGs.

Humanitarianism is synonymous with Volunteerism. It is defined by ethic of kindness, deep sympathy and corresponding action shown to human beings who are in dire need of the basic necessities of life. It is imbedded in benevolence to alleviate the suffering of the people who are in serious lack and are looking up to fellow human beings for succour. The World Humanitarian Day is celebrated every 19th day of August.

The resolution for Humanitarian day by the United Nations was fired by intense sympathy for the less-privileged, the downtrodden, the affected and the victims of calamities, crisis and disease outbreaks. While part of the motive of the day is to commemorate those who lost their lives in the course of rendering humanitarian services, the day is also meant to celebrate the spirit that inspired humanitarian work around the world.

Undoubtedly, humanitarian tasks are the riskiest of endeavours; because their duty post consists of same location that has in the immediacy, threatened the life of the persons that are being rescued or revived. For instance, against all odds, humanitarians break through doors and roofs amid raging fire to rescue a child in a building. They dive into a stormy river to rescue a drowning woman. They land in battlefields to distribute relief materials to the affected, and to cart the wounded away for emergency Medicare.

Indeed, rare group of people stands up for humanity and such people are known as Messengers of Humanity. Messengers of Humanity are individuals who are celebrated for their noble spirits in humanitarian efforts. They stop at nothing to ensure that people at the lowest ebb of socio-economic livelihood are uplifted to have a new lease of life.

Messenger of Humanity, aside from their rescue efforts, also intervene in psychosocial supports for the traumatised, the vulnerable groups, those challenged in health, the widowed and aged. The emergency situations created by the terrorists' insurgencies and disease outbreaks are instances that humanitarian efforts hold sway.

Humanitarians, obviously, answer the call to duty by God, by bringing smiles to the faces of battered and shattered individuals, in defiance of the intents of the inflictors of pains, such as the insurgents and diseases. In fact, the life of the humanitarians epitomises that of Jesus Christ who came according to the Book of John "that they might have life and that they might have it more abundantly".

Vulnerability is a multidimensional phenomenon that describes the inability of class of individuals in the society to withstand the adverse impacts from multiple stressors, namely abuses, social exclusion and natural hazards that they are exposed to. Ironically, social forces, institutions and cultural values exert this impact on individuals whom they are supposed to sustain.

This menace has numerous dimensions such as, child vulnerability, social vulnerability, environmental vulnerability, to name but a few. One thing is sure; they portend lack of access to the basic necessities of livelihoods: necessity of food, necessity of shelter, necessity of freedom of expression and necessity of association. Vulnerability breeds the various societal ills such as child labour, street hawking, prostitution, armed robbery, and other antisocial activities rampant in our society today.

CHAPTER 9

Robust Economy & Sustainable Livelihood

Imagine a world of only two countries, which have to transact commodities since none is completely self-sufficient. Now, country A is richly endowed and has been able to harness its resources optimally, while country B is less as organised. Assuming country B needs to import 10 units of items from country A and have to export 1 unit of item as valuable as the commodity it imported, ratio of export-import is 10:1. The foregoing scenario underlies the principle of Balance of Payment (BoP). In the above, ratio is in favour of country A which literarily represent what the exchange rate is. This translates to N10: $1 exchange rate, assuming these are the monetary units concerned (say, between Nigeria and USA).

In a nutshell, country's value of currency is determined by quantity of its exports vis-à-vis import, thus the more country exports; the stronger its currency. In the long run, however, the direction may change, because as price of currency increases, the demand decreases causing a downward trend of the value of such currency. At this point, devaluation of the currency becomes pertinent.

Devaluation of currency is the action of the Central Bank to reduce the value of its currency below the market price. This is economic engineering, the exchange rate is momentarily reduced against the standard arbiter (dollar) to prep the demand of domestic goods and services exported, occasioned by reduction in price of such exported commodities. Notice, that this is precipitated by the devaluation policy. Point of caution is that those goods must have price elasticity of demand.

It is simple to observe that to shore up foreign exchange rate, adding value to domestic produce is necessary to increase its exportation value. Since Nigeria's mainstay is agrarian, for example, the adoption of industrial cluster approach is necessary. This approach has remained effective because array of the advantages it offers. Machineries can be obtained collectively and used by members of the cluster. Government conveniently provide infrastructural assets in the cluster for optimal usage. The former may be motivated by the volume of tax generated from such investment due to huge population. With this opportunity, hitherto raw materials will be transformed, even to a semi-nature to raise its value.

Although, economic integration is within the purview of the national government, effective integration is a robust strategy at the disposal of states to address common concerns of their area. Events and experiences have proven the efficacy of this approach. Indeed, growth and development are the outcomes of this effort; as such it is a highly commendable investment because of the quantum of change that effective regional integration creates. Primarily, the motive for this commitment is to engender peaceful coexistence drawn from economic stability. This translates to sustainable development of states and industrial transformation of localities. Peaceful coexistence, therefore, is a valuable asset for economic growth.

In view of effective group integration, North Atlantic Treaty Organization (NATO), an intergovernmental alliance, comprising countries in the Northern America and Europe, sometime, took a stand to curtail the uprisings and insurgency that have threatened its members, especially in East Ukraine. In the Wales

Summit of NATO, where the resolutions were taken; the terror in Northern Iraq by the resistance group was also condemned. In the same manner, EU also stepped up strategies in sanctioning erring members in terms of peaceful coexistence, and to match external aggression. ECOWAS, the foremost West African sub-regional group, has undoubtedly held sway on the fight against insurgency and diseases in the region, especially the Boko Haram attacks and Ebola outbreak.

The justification of this position hinges on the proven efficacy of strength in effective integration and collective responsibility. Ordinarily, the mentioned challenges would be herculean for a single country to grapple with, hence the clarion call for member states in intelligence sharing and stepping up of trainings in counter-insurgency to stem the challenges. ECOWAS has voiced out the counter-productive nature of border closure of member states in a bid to check outbreaks of Ebola disease in sister states. Of course, West African sub-region has meanwhile, proven its mettle in view of their effort to fighting the Ebola Virus Disease and terrorism. These threaten humanity, peaceful coexistence and meaningful progress.

Therefore, Nigerian should take advantage of its membership to these various groups to step up fight against insurgency and disease outbreaks. Furthermore, as integrations in the sub-regions are strengthened, meaningful intents and efforts should be geared towards economic support and opportunity creation through improvement of market access and increased aid for growth among member states. This is expedient, because the appreciable level of buoyancy of member governments guarantee their resilience over external and internal aggressions.

The roles of the state governments and federal government alike, as laudable as they are, require private sector participation to close up the gap existing in the tertiary education industry. The federal government after determining the capacities of the private entities that propose to establish universities, and number of candidates who are denied admission into institutions of higher learning due to lack of admission vacancies, it considered the involvement of the private enterprises in that sector. The response has been magnificent. Definitely, the advantages that the enactment of establishment of universities offer outweigh the disadvantages, considering the enormous difficulty prospective university candidates encounter and the measure of pressure facilities in existing universities bear to accommodate supplementary students.

Economic revival is at home with both the government and the opposition. The corpus of economic revival has form the standard measure of performance. At what much have you been able to peg the exchange rate and at what digit have you been able to steady unemployment rate? After the pursuit of economic revival, we expect a welfarist state as a result, not knowing that these face opposite directions. Revival is capitalism while welfarism is communism. But in any case, we try to strike a balance between the two. As such to remove or not to remove fuel subsidy fall into two different divides. In a welfarist climate, the government should provide free commodity for which they have monopoly, but in an environment of market revival, profit and completion are chief.

But Keynes would strike a balance and insist that government participation in business of the economy is vital. Chiefly of these provisions is conduciveness of environment for business. These have been purview of government in Nigeria at all tiers. Abia State has potentials in massive volume. The industrialists Aba is a case in point. The investment in education, especially at the foundational level is commendable. The Friends of Schools Initiative who adopted education for development is a performing investment that will have its effect multiplied into other real sectors.

Incentivisation as a strategy is found in the State. This is necessary for rapid development of areas. The pursuit of development agency portfolios in the state is a step in the right direction to stimulate economic activities especially at the grassroots, which are vital for overall development of the state. The road infrastructure being rehabilitated is a launching pad for accelerated development. Indeed, it drives increased commercial activities, especially in Aba, where that component of developed are long hungered for. Tourism is a viable sub-sector in Abia State. Many of them are not yet discovered and in fact known but not development. Each clan in LGAs are rich with historical scenarios. For example, that some clans are traced along the line of history, interface with fellow clans. Their meeting point and artefacts relating to that could form tourist destinations.

The State has embraced development partnership and PPP. In fact, development partners, like World Bank are amenable to PPP financing in variety of shades, including Turnkey and Greenfield projects. Thus PPP is a vibrant initiative for development and engine for economic growth. In socioeconomic re-engineering, Public Private Partnership has proven to be veritable and effective in outcome delivery for which the people testify and partake in dividends of democracy. Although PPP is relatively new in the arsenals of development specialists, it has grown in leaps and bounds, demonstrable by the government, and the governed coming and reasoning together for the development of the State.

The fulcrum of development in PPP is entrepreneurship and cutting-age specialization. This makes PPP an efficient engine for economic transformation, whereby corporate bodies conjoin with the government to complement efforts in delivering social amenities to the people in rural and urban areas. Couple of arguments has gone forth as to demerits of PPP, but they have not been able to out-weigh the benefits of this initiative. The government gets closer to the people and there is cross-pollination of ideas. Again, since the governed participate in nation building; the task of communicating lessens and feedback mechanism becomes more efficient.

PPP provides framework for which abundant human resources will be galvanized for maximum production. The return on investment accrued to the private and public sectors will be re-invested for further growth and better infrastructural development, consequently. It is important to bring to the fore that Micro, Small and Medium-scale Enterprises (MSMEs) through the initiative of PPP blossom and effect further industrial growth.

Sight should not be lost on the social work sector of the economy because of their track record of contribution to nation building. The civil society has volunteerism as fulcrum for delivery. It is the oil that drives the community development and of course the hallmark of social sector transformation. Volunteerism re-emphasizes the philosophy of sacrifice which is pivotal to nation building. Like never before, Nigeria needs to strengthen the spirit of volunteerism. Now that the attainment of Sustainable Development Goals is the order of the day, volunteerism thus has become useful instrument and strategy for achieving the multiple goals that define the SDGs.

Public Private Partnership describes economic relationship between the public and private sectors. Quickly, one striking merit is because the plenitude of skills available in the states cannot be accommodated by the public sector, PPP therefore brings to fore this cream of expertise for optimal performance the government sector. The efficient performance of government organs, and indeed other organizations, largely hinges on innovation, research & development.

Thus, PPP is a vibrant initiative for development and engine for economic growth. In socioeconomic re-engineering, Public Private Partnership has proven to be veritable and effective in outcome delivery for which the people testify and partake in dividends of democracy. Although PPP is relatively new in the arsenals of development specialists, it has grown in leaps and bounds, demonstrable by the government, and the governed, coming, and reasoning together for the development of the State.

Finally, value chain management is at the core of the attainment of high level prosperity in most emerging countries. Indeed, value addition concept has become an important catalyst for accelerated growth and development. This is the nature of PPP that enables it to reinforce effectiveness and profitability in productive sectors of the government, which are desired dividends of democracy.

That a system is functional is a report of satisfactory performance of the components that make it up. Human body and motor vehicles are good examples. The body of a human cannot be intact when the hand or neck suffers dislocation or injury. A car whose crankshaft or camshaft is faulty cannot be firm and at such, cannot move effectively.

As it is with human body and motor vehicles, so is with governments. Governments have arms, organs, ministries, departments and agencies. The concord performance of all these sum to the perfect functionality of government whether at federal, state or local levels. Even the non-governmental organizations also work in concert with the government because their internal governance and general conduct are dictated by the law of the land.

Essentially, the strength of the whole is also explained by the quality of product and outcomes that stem from individual and collective decisions. But beyond these, it is also measured by the impressions we make on people that we interact with outside.

Taking a cue from the United States of America, the spirit of true patriotism is the most precious commodity of American people. Demonstratively, the manner with which they fondle their national flags everywhere, in cars and offices and homes, are glamorous that even people of other nationalities desire to belong.

That spirit is essential in the State for speedy growth. The use of public facilities should bespeak true citizenship and social responsibility partaken with utmost honesty. With the individual and corporate strengths galvanized for united purpose of state and nation- building, the trajectory of Abia for development as a united force will be magnanimous.

We are in the era of transparency and visibility. The digital age, in part, has made it unavoidable. Organizations are obligated by the fashion of internet to display their wares and details for greater sales, satisfactory services, effective communication, and global conformity. But within this atmosphere, the good performers gain, because they stand out firmly. Also, their audience gain as they have value for their effort, interest, money or mandate.

The erstwhile administration in the Federal Ministry of Finance introduced the publishing of Federal Account Allocation Committee [FAAC] disbursement to states. And of course, the present Minister of Finance adopts to continue with this method. Within this scenario, mere speculations of what state government receive are put to rest. And clearly, those who put the funds to good use are justified when you consider what they have delivered as dividend of democracy.

Given the general dwindling economic downturn, state governments have begun to devise alternative means of income generation. Value addition on products through promotion of processing industries in this case therefore becomes imperative to be embraced and with the success of private enterprises, tens of other business concerns will kick-start. As funds are recreated, businesses are buoyant and indeed willing to release part of their revenues as taxes and even as transfers (in consonance with corporate social responsibility) to the government which enhances security and infrastructural provisions.

The subsequent foresight of the government should be vivid. The promotion of agribusiness and perfection of supply chain mechanisms are at priority. This is aimed at adding value at every point of the process line. It is important to note that private-sector-driven approach to enable effective sustenance and value addition are pertinent, because value chain management is at the core of the attainment of a highly prosperous and diversified economy.

Robust economy is not supposed to be built to the detriment of our environment and livelihood. It has persistently been remarked that whereas this campaign is perceived by many as a distance issue, this is in fact a matter at hand that requires decisive action. Therefore, it is pertinent that our daily action should always take cognizance of the enormity of the problem. There is thus, a new persistence in social contract known as environmental procurement.

Environmental Procurement denotes sustainable dimensioning of the process of acquisition of goods and services. It has stuck in the lexicon of procurement practice. The urgency of prevailing environmental issue underscores this innovation and evolvement in procurement framework. Again, it is indicative of donor agencies and governments' growing concern over climate change and related challenges. It is a pointer to the fact that stakeholders in supply chain management, are keen about the wellbeing of citizens regarding habitable, productive and protective environment. Reducing the rates of climate change has been a tumultuous issue. Climate change is a long-time shift of statistics of average weather conditions in localities. It is universal. Whereas climate change could be as a result of normal part of the earth's natural variability, which is related to interactions among atmosphere, ocean and land, as well as changes in the amount of solar radiation reaching the earth, there are natural and human factors of climate change. The natural sources include volcanic eruptions and variations in sun's intensity, while human causes include release of greenhouse gases and changing land surfaces. Greenhouse Effect, caused by greenhouses gases is largely responsible for the globe's climate change, which has serious negative impact on the society. Procurement, thus, is one viable means effective in fighting greenhouse effect, hence the ingraining of the phenomenon into the procurement process.

But importantly, environmental degradation is not limited to greenhouse effect. Soil contamination and use of non-renewable energy are current cankerworms. Incorporation of use of renewable, biodegradable and compostable materials in productions and packaging of procured items will be germane to save our environment. Packaging materials such as reusable and eco-friendly bags, as opposed to non-biodegradable bio-plastic materials and petrochemical based plastics, should suffice in procurement instructions in the bid to conserve our environment.

As noted in the foregoing, Green Procurement describes acquisitions that result to minimal adverse environmental impact. This was innovated to curb greenhouse effect and other environmental challenges. There are now concerted approaches towards reducing elements of environmental degradation through the procurement process. Therefore, some of the issues to be considered while drawing up technical specifications of goods and Terms of Reference (TOR) of consultancies, for example, should include; the energy consumption of products and actions, potential longevity of the system, expandability and recycling design of as well as possibility of reuse, the use of environmentally burdening substance during production phase, noise emission during operations, and take-back and recycling policy of producers of products. Multilateral Development Banks (MDBs), International Financing Institutions (IFIs) and other donor agencies and government institutions indeed have put strategies in place to achieve cleaner environment. Such terms such as Environmental and Social Management Plan (ESMP), Environmental and Social Impact Assessment (ESIA), Resettlement Action Plan (RAP), Environmental Technical Specification, Electronic Products Environmental Assessment Tool (EPEAT), and relevant Eco-Labels can now be sighted in Standard Bidding Documents for goods and civil works of MDBs.

It has become the current practice that bidders are expected to submit comprehensive and concise Environmental, Social, Health and Safety Management Strategies and Implementation Plan (ESHS-MSIP). Contractors are usually required to submit Code of Conduct that ensures compliance with the Environmental, Social, Health and Safety provisions.

In the final analysis, the tenets of procurement should be the bedrock of the process to sustain the traditions that uphold procurement principles. The Tenets of procurement consist of due process, fairness, economy, efficiency, transparency, competition, openness, profitability and productivity. The underlying expectation is that these tenets will imbed sustainable development, especially in the developing countries through the philosophy of Value for Money (VfM).

The term Due Process has become a household term since the turn of the century when public procurement effectively was introduced into the country at the wake of the current democratic dispensation. No doubt, this process has positively impacted on the economy and the mind-set of the citizenry. More importantly, the consciousness of law existing to protect public funds from mismanagement and embezzlements is noble and has helped the nation beyond measure. Due process mechanism implies domestication of international best practices in activities of government and non-government, and imbedding of this system in workstations will not only plug leakages, enhance efficiency and promote having value for money, but will also, enhance the corporate image of the nation to the outside world. Expectedly, the outline of due process framework is encapsulated in the tenets of procurement, which include the pursuit of fairness, economy, efficiency, transparency, competition, openness, profitability and productivity. These tenets support a knowledge driven economy achieved through deconstruction of the unsustainable traditional ideas.

The transportation and logistics sub-sector has a critical role to play in ensuring compliance with green procurement and indeed having real value for money. Their roles range from advocacy for legislation to support for implementation. This is because effective accomplishment of procurement process heavily lies on the successful delivery of goods, civil works and services bargained for. As particularly these goods and civil works (mainly, its goods component) depend on logistics and transportation sub-sector for actual supplies, a regulatory function for green procurement assigned to same becomes justifiable. Of course, this function will be practical and realistic when the transportation and logistical angles of the process are efficiently and professionally handled within the array of transportation modes and nodes. The array of transportation modes and nodes include Sea-Freight (seaport), Air-Freight (airport), Overland (bus terminals, bus-stops, and railway stations), Post and Multimodal.

CHAPTER 10

The Concluding Summary

Economic nosedives and risings, are commonplace realities as far as world economies are concerned. Theories commonplace support this pattern of periodic booms and troughs occurring randomly amongst comity of countries. But the strength of shock-absorbers to ensure long-term stability distinguishes serious economies from the other divide.

Indeed, the robustness of economy goes beyond nominal economic realities but entrenched in the psyche and resilience of the fabrics of the systems. The acquisition of skills and the quality of skills in terms of versatility and turgidity is critical to the robustness of the economy. The stabilizers as economic mechanisms to avoid boom (avert inflation) and avoid depression (avert doldrums) have been effective but do not guarantee robustness of economies, in the real sense of the term.

Therefore, this text has been able to look at the efficacy of industrial-cluster practice as an economic approach, expansionary outlook and attitudinal renewal as an enduring mechanism to achieve economic stability of nations. The former is key in expanding the economic assets, while the latter turns around the perception of the countries to enable radiation of modernisation necessary for sustainable development and industrialization. This discourse however zeroes in on industrial-cluster model and its merits.

Location of production units of economic system has been, for centuries, a thing of keen and diligent consideration. As at global level, governments talk and aspire for an enabling environment in order to attract foreign direct investment, so also, manufacturing outfits seek vibrant environment that optimizes performance metrics.

Particularly speaking, in planning for location of industries, entrepreneurs envision such benefits accrued from nearness to sources of raw materials, availability of skilled manpower, proximity and reliability of power sources, existence of access roads, accessibility of micro-financings, and tax incentivization. In an economic climate characterized by lean resources, these are obviously objects that determines the reality of profit maximization. Hence, the need for similar industries to be located in a place to enable one-service for all benefit. The approach of industrial cluster framework becomes more efficient. Indeed, industrial cluster approach has passed its litmus test in industrialization process in Aba, Abia State of Nigeria, for example.

Further, localization is a policy framework in economic firmament with key outlook of closeness to the market. The viability of providing financing to entrepreneurs in cluster framework has proven effective because the webbed membership makes it difficult for default. The social inclusivity steers the spirit that retain faith on achievement. More so, the positive externalities --the pull effect (agglomeration effect) generates is very profitable. This concept definitely pulls necessary inducement for government to have confidence in the members of the cluster, as have been witnessed in Abia State that enabled the government to send members of the shoe makers' cluster to China to enhance their skills and boost productivity.

The State has broken through this initiative, which have resulted in the high productivity that enable high volume sales of shoe and fabric products to the force and the paramilitary agencies in the country.

Stimulus are essential in the dynamics of economic development. They propel speedy growth of economic indices. Proof of stimulus in the economy, which abound in the enriched discipline of quantum economics, are high velocity of commercial activities, and the viability of these stimulus are evidenced by tangible results in the form of economic expansion. Again, what is most visible in the situations described are increased demand of products and increased income leading to increased savings. Two essential facts have been raised in the foregoing scenarios, increased output and increased rate of savings. The existence of these economic indicators suggest increased rate of growth in the economy, which are largely occasioned by growth stimuli in the system. Incidentally, fast-moving commodities are excellent examples of stimuli.

Nigerian economy requires effective diversification of its economic base. So much so now that the country is facing nose-dive movement in the revenue from the oil sector which should necessitate energy meant to form the bulwark for wealth creation. Again, the potentials for diversification of the economy mainly lie in the domains of manufacturing, agricultural, solid mineral, tourism and the service sectors. Value chain enterprises promote the activities of these sectors. Therefore, value chain enterprises will adequately contribute to the transformation of the nation's economy.

Government provides good economic landscape where abundant human resources will be galvanized for maximization of production. The return on investment will be re-invested in other areas of the economy for infrastructural development, consequently. It is important to bring to the fore that micro, small and medium-scale enterprises (MSMEs), which are part of privately owned businesses, blossom in the an environment where due process is paramount. The due process is an effective economic 'seedlings' for industrial transformation.

Robust economy beckons on a country determined for holistic transformation. The entire sector-sparkplugs must be firing at full blast. The transportation, works, health, agricultural, commerce, trade and education must be steamed. In the transportation sector, the air, land, sea and railways are excellent potentials. Taking railway for example, rail transportation facilitates movement of goods and individuals from one location to another by means of wheeled vehicle that run on rail tracks. The tracks consist of ties and ballast on which the rolling stock, usually fitted with metal wheels, moves. Power is provided by locomotives which either draw electrical power from a railway electrification system or produce their own power, usually by diesel engines.

The contributions of rail systems to the growth of the economies mentioned earlier are spectacular and cannot be over-emphasized. In retrospect, rail transportation during the colonial days was remarked as the colonialist's strategy in exploiting the cash crops and other valuables of the richly endowed colonies especially in Africa. Indeed, railway stimulates agriculture and trade because it provides cheap means of movement of these goods from farm gates to the points they are needed, whether for onward shipment to importing countries or local production. This cycle adds value to the produce because it creates more demands of the raw materials. Of course, when values are added to a farm produce, encouragement is engendered in the agricultural practise which reduces unemployment. Again, as the semi-finished or finished commodities are exported, foreign exchange is earned which bolsters the gross domestic product.

Economic revival is at home with both the government and the opposition. The corpus of economic revival has form the standard measure of performance. At what much have you been able to peg the exchange rate? and at what digit have been able to steady unemployment rate. After the pursuit of economic revival, we expect a welfarist state as a result, not knowing that these face opposite directions. Revival is capitalism, while welfarism is communism. But in any case we try to strike a balance between the two. As such to remove or not to remove fuel subsidy fall into two different divides. In a welfarist climate, the government should provide free commodity for which they have monopoly, but in an environment of market revival, profit and completion are chief.

Incentivisation as a strategy is found in the State. This is necessary for rapid development of areas. The pursuit of development agency portfolios in the state is a step in the right direction to stimulate economic activities especially at the grassroots which are vital for overall development of the state. The road infrastructure being rehabilitated is a launching pad for accelerated development. Indeed, it drives increased commercial activities, especially in Aba where that component of development is long hungered for. Tourism is a viable sub-sector in Abia State. Many of them are not yet discovered and in fact known but not developed. Each clan in LGAs are rich with historical scenarios. For example, the some clans are traced along the line of history, interface with fellow clans. Their meeting point and artefacts relating to that could form tourist destinations.

The fulcrum of development is entrepreneurship and cutting-age specialization. This makes PPP an efficient engine for economic transformation, whereby corporate bodies conjoin with the government to complement efforts in delivering social amenities to the people in rural and urban areas. Couple of arguments has gone forth as to demerits of PPP, but they have not been able to outweigh the benefits of this initiative. The government gets closer to the people and there is cross-pollination of ideas. Again, since the governed participate in nation building; the task of communicating lessens and feedback mechanism becomes more efficient.

BIBLIOGRAPHY

Berry, T. K., Bizjak J. M., Lemmon M. L. & Naveen L. (2006). Organizational Complexity and CEO Labour Markets: Evidence from Diversified Firms. Journal of Corporate Finance, 12(2006) 797-817.

Caplice, C. (2006). Inventory Management: Material Requirement Planning. Cambridge: Massachusetts Institute of Technology.

Goossens, D. R., Maas, A. J. T., Spieksma, F. C. R and Van De Klundert, J. J. (979). Exact Algorithm for Procurement Problems under a Total Quantity Discount Structure. Administrative Science Quarterly, 24,570-581.

Griffin, R. W. (2005). Management: Theory and Practice. Boston: Houghton Mifflin.

Hague, P. (2006). A practical Guide to Market Research. Surrey: Grosvenor House Publishing Limited.

Ijaiya, G. T., Bello, R. A., Adeyemi S. L. & I jaiya, M. A. (2008). The Millennium Development Goals and Socio-Economic Indicators in Nigeria, Indian Journal of Development Research & Social Action, 4(1-2), 29-37.

Ilies and Cavrea(n.d). The link between Organizational Culture and Corporate Performance- an Overview

Kotter, J. P. and Heskett, J. L. (1992). Corporate Culture and Performance. New York: The Free Press

Lukinykh, V. F. and Lukinykh, Y. V. (2015). Algorithm for the Procurement and Inventory Management in the Distribution Supply Chain in 15th International Scirntific Conference Business Logistics in Modern Management. Osijek, Croatia, 79-91

Moharana, S. M., Murty, J. S., Sahoo, D. K. and Khuntia, K. (2011). eProcurement and Purchase Algorithm for Supply Chain Management. International Journal of Internet Computing, 1(2), 43-56.

Nelson, R. M. (2017). Multilateral Development Banks: US Contributions FY2000-FY2012. RS20792: Congressional Research Services (CRS) Report.

Nwachukwu, C. C. (2006). Management: Theory and Practice. Port-Harcourt: Africana-First Publishers

Nwachukwu, C. C. (2009). The Practice of Entrepreneurship in Nigeria. Port-Harcourt: Davidstones Publishers

Punia, B. K. and Luxmi (2005). Organizational Culture in Service Sector: An Exploration. Delhi Business Review. Volume 6, No 1, January-June, 2005, p. 45-51

United Nations Development Project (2008). Environmental Procurement, Practice Guide. (2), Bureau of Management, Procurement Support Office, UNDP

Vrat, P. (2014). Materials Management. Springer Texts in Business and Economics: Springer, India.

Wallace J., Hunt J. & Richards C. (1999). The Relationship between Organizational Culture, Organizational Climate and Managerial Values. The International Journal of Public Sector Management, 12(7) 548-564

Wikipedia (2017). Moharana, S. M., Murty, J. S., Sahoo, D. K. and Khuntia, K. (2011). eProcurement and Purchase Algorithm for Supply Chain Management. International Journal of Internet Computing, 1(2), 43-56.

Wikipedia (2017). Market Research,

World Bank (2014). Guidelines: Procurement of Goods, Works and Non-Consulting Services. Washington DC., USA

World Bank (2014). Guidelines: Selection and Employment of Consultants: Under IBRD Loans and IDA Credits and Grants by World Bank Borrowers. Washington DC., USA

World Bank (2017). Standard Procurement Document: Request for Bids: Works (Without Prequalification). Washington DC., USA

World Bank (2017). Standard Procurement Document: Request for Bids: Goods (One-Envelope Bidding Document). Washington DC., USA

World Bank (2017). Standard Procurement Document: Request for Proposals: Consulting Services. Washington DC., USA

ACKNOWLEDGEMENT

It is only heart-warming for me to acknowledge those whose ideas, notions, thoughts, critics, overtly or covertly, shaped the concept of this book. Undoubtedly, these individual inputs are not only germane to the preparation of this material but critical in building the ideologies that underpin it. Whereas the list may be too long and inexhaustible, efforts are pertinent to recognize as many as memories can avail. This section, therefore, is primeval because it inclines to rewarding and acknowledging the real makers of this text. Granted, I take responsibilities of any error that appears in this book, but their contributions are deep-rooted and cannot be fully recompensed.

Hindsight on my writing effort witnessed early days of attempts to write creatively and crisply. Way back, inspirations abound, fiery and were akin to renaissance, now, not occurring at the Mount Olympus, but in a human entity. No gainsaying that each and every one of us will every now and then experience this episode in their lifetimes. Some may be taken advantage of, while some may be not. Some may be more pronounced than the other; but they undoubtedly occur.

I am grateful to such priceless personalities as Dr O. O. Madukwe, Elder Richard C. Nwala, the Permanent Secretary, Abia State Ministry of Works; Emeka Ononiwu, Coordinator of Donor projects, Mr Nkwachukwu Agomoh, the Permanent Secretary, Abia State Ministry of Health, Engr. Izuchukwu Onwughara, State Project Coordinator, Abia NEWMAP and such institutions as Nigeria Institute of Management (Chartered), Chartered Institute of Logistics & Transport (CILT), Nigeria Institute of Public Relations (NIPR), and Institute of Chartered Economists of Nigeria (ICEN).

My family members who exhibited understanding while this text was put together deserve appreciation and special mentioning. My wife, Mrs Ugonma Nwokoma and my children, Faith, John, Gospel, Seth, and Exalt have been wonderful. Also, worth acknowledging is my mother, an epitome of industry, Mrs Beatrice Nwokoma.

My acknowledgements also heartily extend to my bosom friends, Mr Samson Dele Idahosa, an International Procurement Specialist with the Government of Afghanistan, Dr Uchenna Onyebuchi of UNDP, Abuja, Mr Kingsley I. Uwaga of Abia NEWMAP, and Mr Hassan Opaluwa of Kogi NEWMAP, Prince Anthony Onyeomereneche, the GM of Abia Newspaper and Publishing Company (ANPC), and Mr Uzoma Isiakpu, Director of Information, Ministry of Works are also hereby appreciated.

During my early days in development sector, Dr Greg Osubor of African Development Bank was a shining light in project management. Needless to say, the climate of Abia NEWMAP inspires priceless ideations for which I am thankful to God. The entire State Project Management Unit (SPMU) of Abia NEWMAP is hereby appreciated.

My gratitude also respectfully goes to the Government of Abia State, as proudly being governed by Dr Okezie Victor Ikpeazu, for her ingenuity in industrial-cluster innovation which provided seedbed for this discourse.

Nwokoma, Gibson Anozie
November, 2019